D0897656

*Incredible*
*Good Fortune*

# Incredible
# Good Fortune

NEW POEMS

*Ursula K. Le Guin*

SHAMBHALA
BOSTON
2006

SHAMBHALA PUBLICATIONS, INC.
Horticultural Hall
300 Massachusetts Avenue
Boston, Massachusetts 02115
www.shambhala.com

© 2006 by Ursula K. Le Guin
"November Birds"; "Not Rocks"; "There, Here, at the Marsh"; and
"Rockjack" first appeared in *The Grove Review.* "American Wars" first
appeared in *Poets Against the War,* ed. Sam Hamill, 2003. "Invocation,"
"Nine Lines in August," "Talk Shows," and "Old" first appeared in
*PoetryMagazine.com.* "An Afternoon in Winter in England" and "Watch-
ing the Fractal Set" first appeared in *Lady Churchill's Rosebud Wristlet.*
"In Harney County" first appeared in *High Desert Journal.*

9 8 7 6 5 4 3 2 1

First Edition
Printed in the United States of America
⊛ This edition is printed on acid-free paper that meets the
American National Standards Institute z39.48 Standard.
Distributed in the United States by Random House, Inc.,
and in Canada by Random House of Canada Ltd

Designed by DEDE CUMMINGS DESIGNS

Library of Congress Cataloging-in-Publication Data
Le Guin, Ursula K., 1929–
Incredible good fortune: new poems / Ursula K. Le Guin.
p. cm.
Includes index
ISBN-13 978-1-59030-314-6 (acid-free paper)
ISBN-10 1-59030-314-8
I. Title.
PS3562.E42I53 2006
811'.54—dc22
005026695

# CONTENTS

## *Notes from a Cruise*   39

## *Histories*   57

## *Silence and Speech*  77

## *Index of First Lines*  93

# A Note to the Reader

We all knew that being a writer was as lonely a job as being a lineman in Nevada. But we also knew that, after work, famous writers got together. They clumped. Vergil and Horace and that lot in Rome were buddies, Coleridge and Wordsworth took forty-mile strolls together, Byron hung out with Percy and Mary, Bloomsberries fell in love with Bloomsberries, satirists snarled at one another at the Algonquin, beatniks clumped in buses. And the rest of us, the lonesome, non-famous writers, envied them. We wished we could talk shop, talk about writing with people who wrote. We wished we could show our manuscripts not only to editors but to fellow writers, whose judgment might be more collegial and less conventional. But unless you could parlay yourself into a writing retreat, how did you find other nonfamous writers to clump with?

Authorial isolation suddenly decreased with the invention of the peer-critique workshop style of teaching writing. People went home from such workshops and formed spin-off groups, from which other groups budded fractally. Now almost every city and town has some kind of writing cell: writers, from amateur to pro and all stages in between, who meet regularly to exchange their writing, criticise and discuss it, talk shop, and whine communally. Now even a lineman in Nevada can join a writing group, at least virtually.

I began teaching such workshops almost as soon as they were invented, and soon joined writers' groups that followed peer-group rules. I have belonged to several. The scariest kind, to me, is a poetry group, but being scared seems to be good for poetry.

I'm one of a small clump of poets that has been meeting monthly for over two years. It is known as the Poultry Group (from how they pronounced the word "poetry" when I was at Harvard). Some of us had published poetry or had been writing it for a while; one, although a published fiction writer, had just started. We agreed that each month one of us would set an assignment for all of us. At first strict exercises in meter and form, by now these have branched out into subject matter. A great many of the poems in this book were written in direct response to these assignments.

The impulse to make a poem can be sparked, and kept from groping in a void, by having a given direction to take. Working in a specific form — tetrameter, sonnet, narrative — though it may begin as mere exercise in artifice, can release unexpected resourcefulness of language, and let self-hidden passion speak. Discipline, mastered, grants freedom.

I wrote poetry before I wrote stories, and ever since; early on, it was almost all in traditional forms, conventional and unexperimental, which I'd absorbed from reading the poets of the seventeenth, eighteenth, and nineteenth centuries. Rhyme and meter were my native poetic tongue. Only as an adult did I come to write the free verse of my own century, and to feel dimly ashamed to use end-rhyme, ballad meter, and such unfashionable devices — though I never quite stopped doing so.

So it was a joy to me to be *required* to write formally — to speak my own dialect again at last. And it was good to be required to try the more formidable forms, and to work more rigorously on rhyme, meter, and pattern, taking it all further than I'd dared go alone.

Two conclusions: first, a peer group may profit by concentrating on craft. Skill and experience in technique, learned by practice and by heeding the criticism and discussion of the others in the group, are solid gain. I think my art has improved; I know I read poetry with a better-informed awe at the art of the great makers.

My other conclusion is ever so original: Better late than never! I was well over seventy when we got our Poultry Group going, and, even if my daughter will always be a pullet to me, none of us is a spring chicken. Age doesn't matter. The poetry is there to be written. We're here to write it.

With loving thanks to Bette, Caroline, Judith, Molly, Noel, and Shelley.

*Ursula*
*August 2005*

*A Book*
*of*
*Songs*

## The Old Lady

I have dreed my dree, I have wooed my wyrd,
and now I shall grow a five-foot beard
and braid it into tiny braids
and wander where the webfoot wades
among the water's shining blades.
I will fear nothing I have feared.
I'm the queen of spades, the jack of trades,
braiding my knives into my beard.

Why should I know what I have known?
Once was enough to make it my own.
The things I got I will forget.
I'll knot my beard into a net
and cast the net and catch a fish
who will ungrant my every wish
and leave me nothing but a stone
on the riverbed alone,
leave me nothing but a rock
where the feet of herons walk.

## The Housewife

I will follow the meter man
and read the whirling dials
hidden on houses by bushes,
O sweet Peter my meter man!
The dials go creepwhirling round and round.
Thrushes are chuckling under the bushes.
Here comes the postman walking his miles
round and round, over the ground,
brave Daily Bailey my maily man!

I will destroy the dials with you,
I will lose the letters with you,
Peter the Reader, Bailey-go-gaily,
only be true to me, only be true.

# The Girl at the Gate of Fairyland

Were it only I and Oberon,
the old tale would take a new turn.
Titania and Tam Lin, some trim lad
it always is, she aching after him,
the Queen and the commoner. Then something
                                    queers it,
her fancy fades, she finds a new one,
and Tam's on the hillside, heavy-hearted,
palely loitering, dead leaves in his pocket.

But riding past on their pale roans,
if the Elf Lord, not the lady,
looked aside, if he saw me see him,
if our eyes met, oh, my mortality
would strike him to his heart's socket,
till glad of grief he grasped at life
and left his kingdom for my quick lands,
to stand as day outstared the dawn
hand in hand with me on the hillside,
to learn the lovers, not their love, will die —
if it were only Oberon and I!

# The Shiksa

My joyful Jew, my jubilant Jew,
my young King David, an ear so true,
I would have given the world for you.
Why did you listen to elderly voices
telling you how to limit your choices?

> 88 piano keys.
> 44 today.
> 22 tomorrow.
> Now the only key you play
> the sour note of sorrow.

No music under the bigotries.
The tie that binds untied us,
divinities divide us.
Sheep to that side, this side goats.

Still, kneeling on my knobby knees,
I hear the holy psalms, the notes
of 87 silent keys.

# The Drowned Girl

My head is wet
My head is wet

Something
Something
I forget

I did not want to wash my hair

Something terrible
unbearable
or maybe not

Sometimes babies are born dead

It doesn't matter
in the water
what I wanted or forgot

## The Forsaken Shepherdess

I love to sit beside the stream
that runs so fast and fiery,
setting the forest trees aflame
with the joy of its desiring.

I watch the fishes of the stream,
the blinding trout, the blazing carp,
and hear its music go and come,
plucking the incandescent harp.

I'll sit beside the lava stream
as my lambs leap and gambol
like molten clouds at sunset time,
flocking crimson, fleeting nimble.

I'll pipe my tune of joy and shame,
a simple shepherdess alone,
while slower, blacker runs the stream
and all the lowlands turn to stone.

# The Mute

What song will she sing
who is dumb? She can hum
like bees, she can rustle
like the trees, like the birds
she can whistle, anything
but words.

Why is she so?
Her human tongue was cleft
by a feathered arrow. The dark sparrow,
the judgment crow, the anger owl
split her language, left
her to trill and hiss and howl.

Standing near her
I sing for her
words of fear
and hope and horror.

## The Lorelei to Heinrich Heine

I don't know why I am so sad.
I watch the river ships go by
and see a harmless sailor lad
and call him and he comes to me
into my arms to die
and we sink down and down
he to drown, not I,

for what I breathe is not the air
when I sit lonely in the sun
and comb my hair and comb my hair
till there comes by another one,
some boy a mother had,
to sink with me and die.
O why am I so sad?

## The Woman in the Attic

I am the mad woman in the attic,
professionally frantic. Hear my laugh?
Loud, singularly mirthless, automatic.
I am the first and worthless wife.

My heart is not in this poem.
How could it be? My life
is contingent, like that of the Golem
or the Golden Calf,

on a word written on my forehead,
or a popular belief.
I am boring, I am bored.
Ha ha I say to joy, ha ha to grief.

# Anonyma

When the great lordly singers hush,
my casual and selfless voice
that takes no profit, makes no choice,
pipes up, indifferent as a thrush.

When brazen monuments corrode
and praise is dust in dust with blame
and dateless night hides every name,
I still go lilting down the road.

It's sad that hopes and poets die,
but my dear task and fondest care
is to bear softly what's to bear
and ever to sing the lullabye.

# The Little Girl

When Mother sends me to see Gran
    I wear my old red hood
and walk as fast as ever I can,
    trit-trotting through the wood.

And when I see the Wolf in bed
    in Granny's flannel gown,
he says the things he's always said
    and gobbles me right down.

Inside his gut I play my drums
    and Granny plays her sax,
until the noble Woodsman comes
    and splits him with an ax.

Then she and I come crawling out
    all bilious and gory,
and listen to the people shout
    and tell the hero's story.

He smiles modestly; they cheer;
    and I trot home alone,
and nobody will ever hear
    Little Reddy Ridey Roodey on the
        drumbarumbarumba
        and Great Gut Granny on the alto saxophone.

# The Woman in the Basement

I am the woman in the basement
singing singing very low
so nobody hears me at my magic casement
opening on nowhere to go.

I am the old old old old woman
dug halfway into the ground
forgetting to be nice and to be human
fingering the treasures I have found:

the booby rubies and the faded jade
the lying diamonds and the true moon stone.
Here underneath my house I'm not afraid.
I've already counted all the bones.

Ulna, Humerus, Rib, Toe, Skull:
You're no more me than I am you.
You're discrete and pure and dull.
I am innumerable and askew.

Long years past birth I multiply.
I populate the universe.
Scattered stars in earthen sky,
I am all the Ancestors.

*Season*
*and*
*Place*

## Incredible Good Fortune

O California, dark, shaken, broken hills,
bright fog reaching over the beaches,
madrone and digger pine and valley oak,
I'm your dryhearted daughter.
I listened when the earthquake spoke
and learned what the quail teaches.
The stony bed the rain of winter fills
waited all year for the water.

# San José Palms

Palms
in seawind
licks of light
flickers, flashes
clicketing of high
fronds, dry streaming
water-clatter, windsound
rattle-rustle of the air-trees
the sway-trees, the calm trees

# NOVEMBER BIRDS

## Geese

In the black dark morning early
laughter high up through rain,
cloud-coyotes cackling,
hollering, let's go let's go!
go geese! skyhounds, south-streamers,
wild hearts over house roofs,
shivering skeins, broken necklaces,
hundred, hundreds this autumn daybreak
unwriting dark words in long lines,
crossing out our ways and highways.

## Crows

They came in their usual black
unusually silent, sat
on one branch or another,
shifting about, uneasy,
as if the funeral was late.
Dead ivy smothered
their ruinous chapel.
One by one they took flight
heavy, reluctant.

# Juncos

The small folk of the cold
have followed the fall
of mercury down
the slant bare hills of air
and the swift wind-river
here to low ground.

## Winter Days

I am so heavy with mortality
I cannot lift my hand
to take the day, but drift and dream,
forget the dream, and drift again.

Hanging like silt in stagnant pools
or clouds that hold their rain,
I lapse from sleep to half-sleep
and wonder that I wake.

Such sleep is like a tideless sea,
deep beyond depth, and wide enough
to hold the dust of galaxies
and the far bright isles of life.

Tideless, yet the currents run
soft where the light drops soft
through blue to darkness, and again
level I hang, and dream, and drift.

# QUATRAINS

## November

    My feet in cold shallow sea waves
Make the rustle of dry leaves.
    My feet in red fallen dry leaves
Make the plashing of sea waves.

## Fulfilment

Tonight to be entire: the East and West,
wind-driven spar and entered air,
rough hollow hand and full soft breast,
mouth, teeth, tongue, and juicy pear.

## Song Sparrow Song

Hear him so sweetly
start to repeat it,
pause and complete it
    freely, freely, freely!


## Song

Light as the fog lies over the water
    Love lies on my breast.
Never a lover or son or daughter
    Lay so deep at rest.

## On Hemlock Street

I see broad shoulders,
a silver head,
and I think: John!
And I think: dead.


## A Valentine for Krakie

    In the house of the sunrise
hangs a lamp of white shell.
    In the houses of dust and darkness
a woman wearing turquoise laughs.

## An Afternoon in England in Winter

At a quarter to Edward, the late post
slides out of the opening, undulant.
"When are you doing?" the clock asks.
"Tenzing," I answer, nervously expectorant,
spitting rain across the shingle beach.
A trawler on the murky sea just east
of yesterday drags the dark hours in
along with a few octopus, and Moira.

## Waking in April

Drifting on the birdsong river
between no light and light
and the sleep of a man and a cat,
I wear the soft old shirt
my mother made me seventy years ago,
nightshirt, dayshirt,
winter coat, wedding gown.
I wonder, as it wears away to rags
and gauze, will there be a mirror
to see the naked soul in,
or only an unraveling of shadow
as the day widens
and things grow clearer.

# The Non-Cartesian in June

Sun shines through roses
moving in the wind.

Are the wind the sun the roses
all one?

The sun the roses the wind
one articulate thing?

Questions the mind raises
on a summer afternoon.

Are the sun the roses the mind
one with the wind?

The roses are pale pink.

I am, therefore I think.

# Nine Lines, August 9

The gold of evening is closing,
drawing in, tightening.
The light is losing. It is
a little frightening
how fast August goes.
Others have noticed this.
The cat on his concealed switchblade toes
comes by, and what he says
is silent, but enlightening.

## Mount Rainier from Amtrak

We steal on steel through vague terrains
of sheds and fences, weeds and waste.
Over the jumbled, trashy plains

the mountain lifts its owl-skull face,
immensely silent, blind with sun,
inhabitant of another space,

alien to things that run
on tracks and roads, to scurfs of roofs,
crisscrossing wires, confusion:

enormous and indifferent proof
to passing souls in passing trains
that what can bless us stands aloof.

# Another Weather: Mount St Helens

Weightless clouds and airy rain drift over
a lower, slower weather in the world
where lava turns in vast typhoon pavanes,
thick fire beneath a ponderous earthen sky:
storms brew a thousand years before they break
in quaking thunder of tectonic shift
to hurl their hot bright hail straight up, send forth
the monstrous overwhelming wave, or still
a city into feathery clouds of glass.
    I watch you, my volcano, through the depths
of sunlit air, and see you snowy-flanked
breathing your lazy steam-plume south, yourself
a vapor drifting, a bright veil of stone.

# IN HARNEY COUNTY

## Chapman Point

How often I think of that
strange ridge standing
across the sagebrush range,

an ancient riverbed
now an abrupt wall
dividing levels of desert.

The road zigs up steep
to the steep down zag.
At the top moment

you see the lake
of the white pelicans
and the nothing-much-looking mountain,

Steens, that drops five thousand feet
on the far side, faultblock,
subtle and enormous geology,

structure of my deep joy.

# Rockjack

*For David, who told me the word*

A staveless barrel,
it holds tense
some hundred yards of
barbed wire fence.

Four steel posts
wound with wire
to make a cage
three feet or higher

for a pile of rocks,
a stump of stone,
in Harney County,
Oregon.

A rockjack keeps
places apart.
A good place
for a thought to start.

## 95° in the No Shade

Went footsteps across over head
on flat roof of trailer
crackbone    crackbone    crackbone
three footsteps
desert wind walked
over desert over roof over head
to the beat of the heat of the sun
on dirt on butte in blood in head

Went again three footsteps
bonecrack    bonecrack    bonecrack
smoke blown from fires
in the southeast
dirties wind, eats mountains

Smoke blown    fire blown    drybone
drumstick beats white sun

Trailer been here 40 years
jumps in its tracks
like a whipped horse

## Hot Sapphics

"It's a big one," telephone tells us. "Not close.
Wagontire, and south of the Double O Ranch."
August twilight thickens and slowly gets dark,
     hot and uneasy.

Under Mars that burns like a flying ember,
sunset rises, wrong on the ridgeline: red haze:
burning, burning, sagebrush and rangeland burning.
     Darkness and far fires.


## Some of the Locals

I
Small, wise sheep face.
White circle round dark horse's eye.
Flea-leap.  Deer-lope.
Almost stone stillness.
But the ears, the ears!
Jackrabbit, only you.

II
Spring upwelling, shower of voices,
river of branches, fountain of leaves,
Cottonwood! lift the secret streams

to shiver and brighten, to whisper
water to the bonedry wind.

III

Our rumps are copper and much to be admired
and we perch facing almost all the same direction
on the electrical wire and we look underneath our
                                                    wings
with our beaks for nits and we tell all the gossip
to each other and everybody else every morning
and all over again with additions in the evening
and suddenly fall silent

and suddenly are gone to Mexico


## Up in a Cottonwood

I

Who could have for some reason
put a large grey stone
way up in a cottonwood?
Not even on a branch: a twig
holds up that feather boulder
softer than the evening air.

Another deeper in the leaves
turns its silent horns this way,
gazes, shifts the grip
of the mousedeath talons,
and softly tells us who.


II
Indignant indolence.
Wrath gone all downy.
An awful gold round glare
shut halfway to pure contempt.
    *Birdwatchers.*
*Someone should remove them.*
*If they were smaller*
*If it were evening*
*I would see to it.*
    *And presently*
*issue a pellet containing their bones.*


III
Moon cursive
shell curve
of wings in leaves and shadows
soundless, halfseen.

An owl is mostly air.

# Peace in Harney County

rests in the line of a long, low mountain, blue against
blue,
hangs in the meeting of willow and image of willow
in water,
describes all the sky with the vulture's rapturous,
langorous circle,
sleeps in a whitening deerbone in dust at the fall of
the rimrock.
Peace is the form and the meeting, the soaring, the
sun on the bone.

# The Cactus Wren

*(Joshua Tree National Park)*

In this great silence, to sit still
and listen till I hear the wren
is to draw free from wish and will.

She flits to perch; her slender bill
spouts a thin jet of music; then
in the great silence she falls still.

Wind nods the short-stemmed flowers that fill
the sandy wash. She sings again
her song devoid of wish or will.

The hummingbird's quick drum and thrill
is gone just as I hear it, when
in this great silence all holds still.

The granite sand, the barren hill,
the dry, vast, rigorous terrain
answer no human wish or will.

Again, the small quicksilver trill
that has no messages for men.
In the great silence she sings still
of pure need free from wish or will.

# Notes from a Cruise

*Port Canaveral to Astoria*
*via the Panama Canal*
*April and May 2003*

# I. LES ILES SOUS LE VENT

## The Virgins

Between an ocean and a sea,
under the wind, and all remote,
the high green islands silently
ignore the passing years and boats.
Knowing themselves alone, set free
from continental angst, they float
where only wind and water are,
intrinsically, purely far.

## Their History

An ignorant jungle wreathes its flowers
where fields of sworded sugar cane
glutted the slavers' greed and power
with sweetness pressed from human pain.
Injustice and cruelty are ours
and only ours, and always vain.
The unplowed fields grow wild and calm.
The trade wind whispers in the palm.

## II. Aruba

Twenty by six flat miles wide.
Fancy hotels, resorts and such.
What grows that hasn't halfway died
is scabbed and spiny to the touch.
The Spanish, French, and British tried,
gave up, and left it to the Dutch
to slave and mine and process oil.
There really wasn't much to spoil.

## III. The Coup de Grace

The frigate bird with forkèd tail
and the majestic pelican
soar, and flash down from full sail
to persecute the fishy clan.
The beauty of their greed I hail,
their splendid difference from Man.
No clumsy primate feeds his face
in such a stunning act of grace.

## iv. Deck One Infirmary Blues

Frogmarched along the corridor
by crewmen and a friend, the gaunt
old man screamed, "Heil Hitler!" — swore,
"I can do anything I want!" —
"Yes, Harold." — "What am I here for?" —
"To calm down." — "I am calm! I can't —
That fucking hag my wife — God damn!
I hope she croaks!" — and the door slammed.

# V. SORCERIES OF SAN BLAS

## The Molas

"I guess you do this sort of thing
if you don't have television," says
the lady tourist, wandering
through narrow alleys all ablaze
with sea-blue, green of parrot's wing,
fire-red, pure gold, a gorgeous maze
of birds and bats and fish in stitches
sewn by tiny, bright-eyed witches.

## Two of Them

The witch with one tooth wraps a cat
in lace: a dollar a photograph.
The hapless cat accepts its fate
with meek despair. The babies laugh.
The shy witch hides behind a mat
of mystic creatures of her craft;
beneath the stitchery nothing shows
but little, brown, expressive toes.

## The Village of Sug Tupu

The one-room huts have outer walls
of bright, enchanted tapestries.
The witches hang their fine-sewn spells,
their labyrinths and mysteries,
their azure toucans, scarlet owls,
a magic, many-colored frieze
to snare the eye, seduce the mind,
and hide the life that's lived behind.

## VI. Antigua: The Silence
   of the Mountain

A long, long line slants up the sky,
half seen half guessed: through milky haze
it draws the eye and draws the eye
higher and higher still, amazed
that silent earth can raise so high
a pure geometry of praise.
But churches bowed and towers broke
the last time the volcano spoke.

## VII. 24 Knots at Night

A level waterfall, our wake
flees flashing white into the dark.
The ceaseless engine-thunder shakes
the mind to silence, and a stark
and starless blackness with no break,
no hint of light, surrounds this ark
that bears across the midnight stream
a thousand sleepers and their dreams.

## VIII. Pelicans

They're awkward, angular, abstruse,
the great beak on a head so narrow,
a kind of weird Jurassic goose
lurching into the modern era.
But the blue arc of sky lets loose —
look, now! — the brown, unerring arrow!
And see how beautiful, how grave,
the steady wings along the wave.

## ix. Passengers

We have all done hard work. The men
have fought their wars and earned their worth,
and now they tell it all again.
The women have been in childbirth
and served the child, the grandchildren,
and done what women do on earth.
Our recompense is blear-rimmed eyes,
wrinkles, bad feet, thin hair, fat thighs.

Unfair, that duty fairly done
should only come to ugliness.
Old husbands offer to the sun
their hairy paunches; old wives dress
in girlish shorts or glittering gown,
all new, as if they hoped to bless
the voyage into seas unknown
with unworn beauty not their own.

Trying to disown or disdain
the foundered hopes our follies hide
with bonhomie that cheapens pain
and boastfulness that perjures pride
and labored fun that wants to feign
no children lost, no friends that died,
we skirmish still as we retreat,
we veterans of the long defeat.

## XIII. 124°30' West

Voyage by sea induces one
to part with certain certainties.
Now California, Oregon,
those uttermost Hesperides,
lie bright beneath the rising sun,
and what was always West is East.
For sometimes Always must be reckoned
by the degree and by the second.

## x. Nobody

You put your glass down anywhere.
It vanishes. The dirty dish,
the sodden towel, disappear.
Fulfilment of the housewife's wish,
the husband's bland assumption — here
nobody has to do the wash.
Nobody, here, is brown, and young.
He smiles, and speaks a foreign tongue.

## XI. Baja

On crescents of bright barren sand
and arid heights of scrub and stone
huge sudden cubes of concrete stand
aloof and gaudy, and each one
proclaims its desert as the land
of milk and honey, Sun N Fun.
Mere water's worthless to us wizards
who live where no one should but lizards.

## XII. The News

A page of snippets from the *Times*
slips daily underneath the door
to keep us up to date on crimes
being committed now on shore,
that other world, those earthy clim
of politics and lies and war.
Out here where winds and water
we cherish our brief ignorance.

## XIV. Mementoes

We carry home a motley hoard:
handpainted bowls, handwoven scarves,
a flowered fish, a whistle-bird,
fantasies sewn by fragile dwarves.
A thing may hold, as may a word,
the long canal, the isles, the wharves
of red-roofed towns, the coasts of dawn
and evening where our ship has gone.

## x. Nobody

You put your glass down anywhere.
It vanishes. The dirty dish,
the sodden towel, disappear.
Fulfilment of the housewife's wish,
the husband's bland assumption — here
nobody has to do the wash.
Nobody, here, is brown, and young.
He smiles, and speaks a foreign tongue.

## XI. Baja

On crescents of bright barren sand
and arid heights of scrub and stone
huge sudden cubes of concrete stand
aloof and gaudy, and each one
proclaims its desert as the land
of milk and honey, Sun N Fun.
Mere water's worthless to us wizards
who live where no one should but lizards.

## XII. The News

A page of snippets from the *Times*
slips daily underneath the door
to keep us up to date on crimes
being committed now on shore,
that other world, those earthy climes
of politics and lies and war.
Out here where winds and waters dance
we cherish our brief ignorance.

## XIII. 124°30' West

Voyage by sea induces one
to part with certain certainties.
Now California, Oregon,
those uttermost Hesperides,
lie bright beneath the rising sun,
and what was always West is East.
For sometimes Always must be reckoned
by the degree and by the second.

## xiv. Mementoes

We carry home a motley hoard:
handpainted bowls, handwoven scarves,
a flowered fish, a whistle-bird,
fantasies sewn by fragile dwarves.
A thing may hold, as may a word,
the long canal, the isles, the wharves
of red-roofed towns, the coasts of dawn
and evening where our ship has gone.

*Histories*

## Buz

At first my impulse was to swat,
but impulse yielded to thought,
or hardly thought, mere fellow-feeling
as I watched it walk across the ceiling.
It's a fat fly, but not obscene,
nor dirty, since the house is clean.
It does not take its meals with me,
but eats them somewhere privately.
As night comes on I see it grow
sleepy with darkness, shy and slow.
With morning light it wakes to zoom
cheerfully from room to room.
And my mind, wandering, follows it,
the whining loop, the pause, the flit,
until it stops somewhere to sit
and wash its hands and clean its eyes
after the custom of houseflies.
Then with a hum it's on the wing,
a small, inhuman, wild thing,
aware of me, as I'm aware
of it. We do not touch. We share
a while the mild summer air.

# LOVE SONGS IN LATE MAY

## May 22

I will spend four days
writing love songs
in a house that's near
but doesn't look at
the sea.
    The first
is to the cat Archibald,
the demure, ceremonious,
innocent, elegant archer
of back, bestower
of affection from aloofness,
too young in wisdom
of death and people:
Mischief, Slantways,
devoutly greedy, gaze of amber,
erratic and indolent silk sherpa
to holy wholly mysterious everests,
I make a lovesong to him,
a gift, a dreamfeather.

## May 23

I have seen material light. It whirled
in beauty, entering and leaving
one of the caves of the sun.
The sun-cave brightens going in, hottens,
could consume the maker's hand
like a feather, leave a whiff of ash.
I watched the maker's delicate long hands
quick turning, smoothing, soothing
incandescence, watched her breathe
into the molten mass and saw
her breath turn into light.
Colors took place in air, and were.
    She cut the new thing free and let it rest,
and shut the doors of the amazing cave
where salt dunes turn transparent
to see the sun through.
This love song is to the breath of the maker
and the hands of the maker of light.


## May 24

Solitude is beautiful, so long
as it's set like an opal
in a ring. Where would I be

unset? A milky
bit of gravel staring at the moon
in the desert of the true
aloneness. You: all you: my gold,
my golden ring,
to you and to the gift of solitude
I sing this song but not aloud.


## May 25

*¡O que hermosa es la lengua castellana!*
A silver darkness like a moonlit night;
currents of the air, cool, warm;
slip and rustle of syllables, streams
that gleam on sandstone under cottonwoods
in late spring evenings. The conquistadors
brought that taut lisp with them, the Indians
shaped it to the sun, the volcanoes. Oranges
are in it, blood-oranges, and swords;
a delicate and wilful subtlety,
and a plain soberness the settlers brought
west from Rome two thousand years ago.
I love it all, but most I love the words
of Spanish when my poets say them,
the wild huntress of the river-isle

and the daughter of wind and angel,
daughter of salt and water, mother of poets
of the Valley of Elqui, of the shadow of Aconcagua.


## May 26

No love song.
My hands have held my mother's hands
turned into ashen feathers
in one of the caves of the sun,
bright womb of our mortality.
No darkness
is what blinds.
    The house
doesn't look at the sea, but listens,
listens, full of sea-voice, like a shell.
Like the small hermit in the shell
I listen to the Pacific,
what it says in the morning to the sun,
what it says in the darkness. No language
I can ever learn. No poem
I can make. No love song. Only listening.

## Passing the Clinic

The old fanatic withered man
humped in his director's chair
is half asleep, his sign aslant.
April, October, he sits there,
doomed by a pitiable fate
to waste his constancy in hate.

I will sing to change his sign:
"You think my child is yours to save,
but it is only ever mine.
And it is buried in my grave
as it was buried in my womb,
the seed of all the love to come."

# At the Feast in the Great Hall

I

A bird flew through the candlelight
above the voices and the jangling harp,
window to window, through
and gone —
    *So our life,* the harper sang,
*a moment between dark and dark.*

II

    My wings
blundered in brightness, my eyes
dazzled, then I was across
and home in wide air and the night.
Only for a moment was I lost.

## The Finding

A woman slowly opens a carved box.
She has come to the dark tower, she has found
the hidden room, and quieted the hound
that guards it; she has picked the rusty locks,
pushed open the reluctant door, and seen
the box among the shadows on its stand.
She lifts it. It weighs little in her hand.
She hesitates beside the fire-screen,
hearing the hound whimper, "Do not open it."
The woven peacocks in the curtains scream:
"To wake will break, to wake will break the dream!"
She draws her breath. She slowly lifts the lid.
Stones and darkness vanish. Nothing is there
but her, the grass, the silent, shining air.

# The Lost Explorer

They were all known and named, the rivers of his
                                                North:
Columbia, Wakiakum, Cathlamet, Deep:
clear, dark, strong-running rivers of the truth.

So he set out, how many years ago, to seek
across uncharted ranges of the mind, beyond
the maps and histories, for rivers no one knows,
that leap from undiscovered springs into the sun.
He found and followed the bright, nameless streams;
                                                he found
past all the lonely plains, the sea to which they run.

He wanders aimless now along the echoing beach
of that long coast outside the compass rose,
and glimpsing farther islands he will never reach,
names their imagined rivers with the names of home:
Cathlamet and Columbia; the Deep; Wakiakum.

# Magellanica

I am the Infanta of the farthest places.
The straits of storm, the coasts of desperation
are my inheritance, the secret marshes,
the upward light of glaciers in the mist.
My prayer is the wide spiral of the condor.
I dance in the skin of the guanaco.

Once your people danced with me.
Now you come as foreigners, to fell
my ancient forests of the austral beech,
to scrape the silver myriads from my seas.

I send my ambassador the albatross
to your courts and councils. He returns in silence.

Extremity is all my strategy.
You will learn what desolation is.
Mine is the great death. After it,
only your plagues, your insect agonies.

## Peace Vigil, March, 2003

The candles flickered in a circle,
behind them faces
full of shadows, behind them
darkness, mild rain, plum blossoms.
Spring night in time of war. A big man
with a big ragged backpack
wandered into the circle and stood
looking around, till somebody
spoke to him, somebody gave him
a candle, somebody lighted the candle.
Then he sat down on the wet pavement
right in the empty center of the circle.
He sat huddled up over the candle,
holding it in one hand and holding
the other hand over it to get warm, and then
he would change hands. Now and then
he looked up around the circle
of candles and shadowy faces and silence
and his look was mild and puzzled.
When the circle turned into people
going home he still sat there
in the rain with his candle.

## Talk Shows

In rush and gush of wordy juice
the torrents of our talking run,
*I say to you, he says to them,*
the sap that swells the human stem.

Listen, listen: a lesser voice,
a whisper of the wind on stone
along the river's drouth-white bed,
the shadow of the word unsaid.

## For Karen

Footprints of the terrible
are fresh all round us, the rattle
of catastrophic grief coils
in the dust of the ordinary day.

    Who's going to answer the telephone?

Stupidities of reassurance
as the claw strikes, the tooth
sinks in, of consolation
as the blind face turns away.

    Who's going to answer the telephone?

## Here, There, at the Marsh

The papers are full of war and
my head is full of the anguish of battles
and ruin of ancient cities.

In the rainy light a great blue heron
lifts and flies above the brown cattails
heavy, tender, and pitiless.

## American Wars

Like the topaz in the toad's head
the comfort in the terrible histories
was up front, easy to find:
*Once upon a time in a kingdom far away.*

Even to the dreadful *now* of news
we listened comforted
by far time-zones, languages we didn't speak,
the wide, forgetful oceans.

Today, no comfort but the jewel courage.
The war is ours, now, here, it is our republic
facing its own betraying terror.
And how we tell the story is forever after.

# 3/3/03

Fog in alders. Alders in fog. The pale rust
catkins clouding, crowding the branches, thin stems
silver, shadowed, thousands of silent harp strings.
    March is the war month.

March the noun, the lion that turns to the lamb.
March the verb of armies and soldiers, goose-steps.
Mars the god, beloved of Venus, Mother
    of alders, of all life.

## An American Etymology

Angering comes out of anhungered,
we hear its quiet whistle.
Better not walk too near the dump.

Reachers are there, and achers.
Acreage and anchorage of the blunt pain,
the arm-stump, the dead thistle.

Anger engenders the forsaken. Handless
they reach out, reach us,
arms of the anhungered, the unfilled,

the starved children
stumbling in the plastic castle.

# April in San José

In a city where men shout across the streets
Shit Shit    God bless you lady    ay Miguel
bark wordless pain like dogs,
roar rage in one dark syllable,
or stand and beat an oak tree with their fists,
or walk ten feet of driveway back and forth
in boots and Nazi cap and steel chains,
or sit and shiver, silent, in the sun,

I steer among the wrecks, the reefs,

through poppies, roses, red valerian,
passionflower, trumpetvine,
camellia, dogwood, foam of plum and pear,
mock orange and true orange,
gold of the Hesperides,
sweetness of freesias, garlands, wreaths
of red and yellow, white and green,
dark fragrance of eucalyptus,
glitter and rustle of inordinate palms.

Through the mockingbird morning
I make my way bewildered,
in the city of ruined men
in the valley of the ghosts of orchards
in the broken heart of California
in the nation of addiction
in the kindest month.

*Silence*
*and*
*Speech*

## Invocation

O silence, my love silence,
I have feared you: my tongue
has rattled on my teeth
dreading to be dumb so long
when I am done with breath.
    And I have needed prattle,
kind blather, and the come and go
of voices, human voices,
the sky whose moon you are,
the ground whose flower.
    But I beseech you come,
now, my love silence, O
reward and freedom, balance
beyond choices, in whom alone is heard
the meditation of the twilight bird
and the never to be spoken word.

# English

I love my native language
the lovely viola
the great advantage

a mouthful of pebbles
a welling of water
crashbangs faint echoes

the word if you can find it
for what is and
what is beyond it

## Dance Song

This breath is not any other breath.
Not breathed before, not breathed again.
In a now without a then
it interleaves me with my death.

So for a moment I am free.
Once I breathe, and only once.
Wind blows me and I dance,
willow leaf on willow tree.

# TWO POEMS FOR JUDITH

## I. Not Rocks

"I like to pick up rocks," I said,
as I did so on the beach.
"No you don't," the poet said.
"I don't?" I said, and she,
with the certainty of poets, said,
"You can't. Rocks are too big to pick up.
What you pick up are stones."

After a while, turning over
these hard matters in my head
and in my hand, I asked,
"Is it all right to call them pebbles?"

She said it was all right.
And we walked on together,
she with unhurried, solid stride,
I with a frequent, furtive dip and snatch.

I love words as well as stones
and wish that I could find the words
to tell her why I spend sweet hours of greed
sitting picking pebbles up,
examining, discarding, a jeweler
in mile-long drifts of riches,

keeping only one or two
to carry home and lose
among the other stones from other days,
other beaches, walks, and years;
or how I love them, all the little stones,
pied and striped, flecked and plain,
smooth or grainy: granite, quartz:
their noble names, their ancient lineage,
their humbleness: how good they are
at being what they are, and staying put,
no matter where, my pocket, house,
the breakers' brutal endless jostle.
They are much older than I am.
Unhurried. Solid. Disparate. Like poets,
they have certainty.

I love these hard matters.


## II. Naming

She's thankful that she doesn't know
the names of birds, because the name
usurps perception of the thing —
at least I think that's what she thinks.

I'm from an archipelago

where word and bird are one and same.
Quick, quick, before the dragon blinks,
to save your life you say the name!

Her courage puts my fear to shame.
I see her lightly entering
that forest where you let them go,
all the labels, ties, and links.

I dare not fly on tacit wing
or burn without a tongue for flame.
I face my silent, riddling Sphinx
with only all the names I know.

## A Lament for My Poultry

There's no more chickens in my yard.
Nobody cheeps or clucks or crows
or squawks aloud, *I found a word!*
Where have they gone, the mockingbird,
the nightingale with her rondeaux,
the noisy chickens in my yard?
I find the silence very hard,
and where I go, the silence goes.
Nobody brings me any word.
I used to get so many, Lord!
to give away, to use, to lose,
from sparrows chirping in my yard,
from dove and thrush and hummingbird
and flaming phoenix red and rose
whose song was sharper than a sword.
But now there's nothing to be heard
but what the wind says when it blows
the dust and droppings round my yard
where I squat pecking for a word.

## Seventy

I've lived the life of man,
the span, the seven ages.

Now my life is out of bounds
and doesn't keep the time.

I'd make sense only to myself,
but wear an older habit.

I'd take my rage unsweetened,
but see: I fall to rhyme.

Oh, how am I metered?

## Taking Courage

I will build a hardiness
    of counted syllables,
asylum for the coward heart
    that stammers out my hours,

an armature of resonance,
    a scaffolding of spell,
where it can learn to keep the time
    and bid what comes come well.

# A Request

Should my tongue be tied by stroke
listen to me as if I spoke

and said to you, "My dear, my friend,
stay here a while and take my hand;

my voice is hindered by this clot,
but silence says what I cannot,

and you can answer as you please
such undemanding words as these.

Or let our conversation be
a mute and patient amity,

sitting, all the words bygone,
like a stone beside a stone.

It takes a while to learn to talk
the long language of the rock."

## Ille

Ride beside me,
sleep beside me,
brother ghost
never born.
Be my guide
when I'm lost
and alone.
From your distance
bring me close
to the bone.
Ride with me where I must go.
Dream in me what I must see.
Be what I cannot be.
Be almost me,
brother ghost.
Let me be other,
almost brother.
Set me free.
Ride beside me.
Sleep with me.

## For Naomi

My mother-body held me tight.
I sucked the flowing world from her,
the sweet air, the warm light,
and she sang sleep to me at night.

There's no more comfort in her breast,
and only distance in her arms.
She no longer holds me close.
"Go on," she sings now, "little ghost."

## Learning Latin in Old Age

I feel so foolish sitting translating Vergil,
the voices of ancient imaginary shepherds,
in a silent house in Georgia, listening
for that human sweetness but afraid,
gathering griefs, my flock of goats
dry-uddered and with evil eyes, around me,
seeking the word that will turn them to eagles
or dry leaves to fly off, begone, the word
not even Vergil knew, who died with his work unfinished.

# Futurology

I cannot break free from these iron stars.
I want the raspberry paw-pads of the fox,
but here are only claws, the Crab, the Scorpion,
great shining signs that slide across the sky.

I want the wisdom ignorant of wars
and the soft key that opens all the locks.
I want the touch of fur, the slant of sun
deep in a golden, slotted, changing eye.

O let there be no signs! Let fall the bars,
and walls be moss-grown, scattered rocks.
Let all the evil we have done be done
and minds lie still as sunlit meadows lie.

# INDEX OF FIRST LINES

I am the mad woman in the attic, 11
I am the woman in the basement, 14
I cannot break free from these iron stars., 92
I don't know why I am so sad., 10
I feel so foolish sitting translating Vergil, 91
"I guess you do this sort of thing, 45
I have dreed my dree, I have wooed my wyrd, 3
I have seen material light. It whirled, 61
"I like to pick up rocks," I said, 84
I love my native language, 80
I love to sit beside the stream, 8
I see broad shoulders, 24
I will build a hardiness, 87
I will follow the meter man, 4
I will spend four days, 60
I've lived the life of man, 86
In a city where men shout across the streets, 76
In rush and gush of wordy juice, 70
In the black dark morning early, 19
In the house of the sunrise, 24
In this great silence, to sit still, 38
"It's a big one," telephone tells us. "Not close., 34
Light as the fog lies over the water, 23
Like the topaz in the toad's head, 73
My feet in cold shallow sea waves, 22
My head is wet, 7
My joyful Jew, my jubilant Jew, 6
My mother-body held me tight., 90

No love song., 63

O California, dark, shaken, broken hills, 17

O silence, my love silence, 79

On crescents of bright barren sand, 52

*¡O que hermosa es la lengua castellana!,* 62

Palms, 18

rests in the line of a long, low mountain, blue
    against blue, 37

Ride beside me, 89

She's thankful that she doesn't know, 83

Should my tongue be tied by stroke, 88

Small, wise sheep face., 34

Solitude is beautiful, so long, 61

Sun shines through roses, 27

The candles flickered in a circle, 69

The frigate bird with forkèd tail, 43

The gold of evening is closing, 28

The old fanatic withered man, 64

The one-room huts have outer walls, 46

The papers are full of war and, 72

The small folk of the cold, 20

The witch with one tooth wraps a cat, 45

There's no more chickens in my yard., 85

They came in their usual black, 19

They were all known and named, the rivers of his
    North:, 67

They're awkward, angular, abstruse, 49

This breath is not any other breath., 81

Tonight to be entire: the East and West, 22
Twenty by six flat miles wide., 42
Voyage by sea induces one, 54
We carry home a motley hoard:, 55
We have all done hard work. The men, 50
We steal on steel through vague terrains, 29
Weightless clouds and airy rain drift over, 30
Went footsteps across over head, 33
Were it only I and Oberon, 5
What song will she sing, 9
When Mother sends me to see Gran, 13
When the great lordly singers hush, 12
Who could have for some reason, 35
You put your glass down anywhere., 51